# REPORT

OF THE

## COMMITTEE OF WAYS AND MEANS

ON THE SUBJECT OF

# DIRECT TRADE.

---

HOUSE—5000 COPIES.

---

MONTGOMERY:

BRITTAN AND DE WOLF, STATE PRINTERS.

1852.

# REPORT.

---

The Committee on Ways and Means to whom was referred, the bill incorporating the Alabama Direct Trade and Exchange Company, have duly considered the same, and believing that there is no one subject in which all our citizens have a deeper or more lasting interest than a speedy and radical change in our import trade, beg leave to make the following report:

The skilful and prudent merchant, in selecting a site for extensive, profitable and durable commerce, will examine carefully the whole surrounding country, consider well its climates, soils and seasons; its valleys, hills and mountains; its vegetable, animal and mineral productions; its lakes, rivers and roads; its bays, seas, gulfs and oceans, with their peculiar currents, tides and winds; look well to the natural disposition, capacity, occupation, wealth, habits and customs, opinions, political, religious and moral, of the whole surrounding population. His interest is identical with the greatest prosperity and tranquility of all his customers. He is, therefore, the natural ally of the best and most stable government.

Civilization, the arts and sciences, first appeared in the East. Their course has been Westward; as the world is but a great national race-ground, in process of time, they will again reach their starting point.

The Israelites, Grecians, Romans, and Spaniards have exeerted a powerful influence on the destinies of mankind. They were all extensive slaveholding countries in their days of progress and power. Nations, like individuals, have their birth, infancy, manhood and old age; like them, they have their peculiarities, their inferior or superior mental, moral and physical power and physical organization; like them, they have their fevers, consumptions, epidemics, and chronic infections, and the good of mankind requires, under certain circumstances, that they should be confined, restrained, punished, and, at times, even *destroyed.* They, too, like individuals, in obtaining or making locations on the earth's surface, have advantages or disadvantages more or less suited to their peculiar mental, moral or physical organization, propensities, habits and occupations. The country we now occupy, before it was discovered by the European race, was admirably suited in all respects, to the wild, savage, roving, destructive propensities of the Indian. By nature, free and idle, he could neither be civilized nor enslaved, without destroying his existence or happiness. In selecting a place of residence, all he desired was a wilderness to rove in, and game to gratify his destructive propensities and furnish his food and raiment.

The African, when left to himself, can only exist and be happy under a tropical sun, where summer is continual, clothing not a necessity, and food can be obtained by little effort from the spontaneous productions of the country. Freedom to him, in a cold climate, is a curse compared to slavery under an intelligent master, in a mild one. In their native country, they are a nation of human beings at rest, and likely to continue so until highly stimulated by some race different in physical organization. If, by pestilence, the whole race in their own country were suddenly cut off, Europe and America would only feel it in an advance on ivory and a few spices. The energetic white European or American requires for the full development of his capacity and disposition, a country possessing all the natural elements of the three great pursuits of civilized man, agriculture, commerce, and manufactures. That country combining all these in the most extensive and compact form, in the most convenient location, is, above all others, the best calculated to promote his own happiness and enable him to be useful to surrounding nations.

The white European, in the course of his progress and enterprise, discovered the American Continent, on parts of which the attempt has been made by legislation to bring the Indian and African up to a political equality with the white man. Political equality necessarily brings about social equality; social equality produces amalgamation. This political and social equality, with the consequent amalgamation, has brought on premature consumption and rapid decay in the whole political and social mass, which threatens to bring about premature dissolution and lasting imbecility.

In our portion of the continent we have, so far, followed a different course. We expelled from amongst us the Indian, and kept the African entirely under our control and direction. We, although in infancy, as to the ordinary age of a government, are already a giant in physical power, with strides so long and rapid as to strike with wonder and admiration, all surrounding nations.

There exists in our system of African slavery, a powerful tendency to elevate, and keep free and independent, the white race. Every citizen within these States sees slavery by color, by name and nature, and from the time he can reflect, sets himself above a slave. So long as lands are low and labor profitable, there is no necessity for the poor white man to become dependent, or a slave. The poor white man, and the slave owner, are alike interested in cheap lands and high wages; their interests are, therefore, identical. There is a powerful tendency in all republican States like our free States, to run into the European system of high taxes to favor particular classes. As population becomes dense, capital puts down the wages of labor and can enslave the laborer.

Great Britain is the first commercial nation of the age, unless we may except our own country. Her commercial power, for many years, enabled her to be mistress of the seas. She is now the first manufacturing country of the world. On commerce and manufactures, all her present political power and greatness depend. Any power capable of striking a death blow at her commerce and manufactures, must necessarily be her superior in any military contest waged with equal campaign material and government skill, to hers. She has a home population of twenty seven millions on a territory about the size of Georgia and Florida, with advantages in position, soil, climate, mineral and vegetable productions, of not more than one half of theirs. Her colonial dominions are scattered over every quarter of the globe in all latitudes. Within them, she has large possessions, devoted to the culture of cotton, rice, sugar and indigo. Every effort within her skill or power, has been exerted to excel our country in the production of cotton. Notwithstanding her cotton region contains a population of more than one hundred millions of free laborers, which she calls her subjects, who are employed at mere nominal wages, so far, all her efforts have proved abortive, and must, regardless of soil or climate, unless she establishes our system of African slave labor. The consequence is, that she is dependent on our slaveholding States for a supply of cotton, on which, to a great extent, depends her commercial and manufacturing prosperity. In order to obtain commercial preference, in the markets of Europe and America, in favor of her colonial commodities, she calls them free labor productions, and, by this device, has succeeded in humbuging a numerous class of short-sighted customers in both countries. She has a company called the "East India Company," who rule and govern her extensive East India possessions. From the force of circumstances, her Canadian colonies are governed with more liberality and justice than any other portion of her extensive dominions. She fears their revolt and our assistance. Her public debt is eight hundred millions pounds sterling, a very considerable portion of which was created to abolish African slavery in her West India Islands, and has resulted in the ruin of the whites and blacks on those islands, and a destruction of their commercial prosperity. To pay the interest on this enormous public debt, as the taxes are levied most heavily on the laboring classes and all goes to the higher classes, a large majority of her population are in a much worse state of slavery than the African race are in the slaveholding States of our Union. To pay this tax and obtain a scanty supply of food and raiment, requires constant labor. If affliction, by disease or old age, disqualifies any from capacity to labor, they are thrown out of doors, paupers, upon public charity. Of this class there are now, in Great Britain, over three millions, and in Europe not less than twenty millions, a living fungus upon European governments. The accumulated miseries flowing from their system of government, keep the population in a feverish revolutionary spirit. To preserve law and order, and collect the heavy taxes, requires in England, a standing army of one hundred thousand men stationed all over her territory; yet outbreaks and insurrections are common occurrences. Notwithstanding all this, it is said Great Britain has the fireest and best government in Europe. We know heavy taxes, and standing armies to collect them and enforce obedience to unequal laws—abject slavery of the masses under the delusive name of free laborers—and an uncertainty in the future to every one, are general over Europe. The wealthy have no security from poverty by revolution, and the poor no security from the cannon, the sword, halter or dungeon, for revolt.

Great Britain, by unequal and inexpedient laws, forced upon her North American colonies the alternative of abject submission to unauthorised aggressions, or manly resistance in defense of their most sacred rights. After ten years unregarded remonstrances, hope was lost, and the sword drawn; the contest appeared an unequal one, but seven years war ended in the complete independence of our original thirteen colonies. It was a great loss of political power and sectional agrandizement to the mother country. To the people of the United States and many others, it has been a far greater gain. They abolished the British system of government which holds the citizens to be subjects and subordinate to the King and other departments of the government, and made the citizens of the respective States, sovereign, and the Governor, President, and Legislative bodies, all subordinate to the will of the people, properly expressed through their conventions.

The love of power and aggrandizement has been, in all ages, amongst individuals and nations, prominent and constant. They are powerful elements in human progress, and it is only when unjust means are used for their attainment, that they should be opposed, checked or stopped. Great Britain made a second attempt to subjugate or check our power, in her last war with us. Failing in both instances, she now seeks to weaken us by attacking and urging others to attack, our system of African slavery.

There are four prominent grand divisions within our present extensive boundaries: our commercial and manufacturing States, with their principal outlets through Massachusetts, New York and Pennsylvania; the agricultural States, with their principal outlets through Maryland, Virginia, North and South Carolina, Georgia, Alabama, Louisiana, and Texas, on the Atlantic and gulf coast; California, with the Bay of San Francisco, and Oregon, with the Columbia river, as their principal outlets on the Pacific.

Whatever may be said of California gold, Oregon's farming capacity, or commercial and manufacturing prosperity in the New England or Northern States, a close examination into the Southern Atlantic, gulf, and Mississippi Valley States, must convince every one that there lies, congregated together, in the most compact form, all the elements, in the highest degree, of agricultural, commercial and manufacturing superiority. The general progress, and power of the Union requires, that the resources of this section be wisely and skilfully directed.

Commerce is the heart of circulation in making exchanges of agricultural and manufacturing productions to the whole population. Any policy of the government or habits of the community that has a tendency to turn commerce out of its natural channels, within the same government, is a drawback on the healthy and vigorous action of the whole system.

Our navigable rivers and lakes have their bluffs, which are natural landings. To those bluffs, roads can be made, with more or less labor, of higher or lower grades. When made, they are more convenient and less expensive for a certain surrounding population, as highways and landings, through which to send off or dispose of their surplus productions, than any other road or landing. The same landing and road is also the most convenient and least expensive, naturally, through which to obtain their purchases of other articles.

Our sea or gulf coasts have their natural landings, all of which possess their relative advantages on account of climate, position, accessibility from the land side by navigable rivers or lakes, and the cheapness and low grade with which rail roads or canals may be constructed, leading from them into the interior, and the capacity of the population for production. These landings also have their relative advantages in bays, harbors, ocean currents and winds, leading off in the most convenient direction for commercial purposes. They are the great landings of foreign and coastwise commerce—the landings for our exports and imports, with the same convenience and pecuniary advantage to the whole community, in having all their foreign supplies directly landed at them, for all those whose convenience or interest requires their exports to be landed there, as the small landings on the rivers or lakes. A system of commerce, to be most convenient and least expensive to the whole community, must necessarily have all its import agents or merchants at their export landings or cities. Any other system is unnatural, inexpedient and ruinous to every interest in the whole community, and a continual drawback on the aggregate prosperity and wealth of the country at large. The first enquiry for every class of every section in every State is, what seaport landing or city on the gulf or coast can be reached at the least expense on products—first, by natural highways, as navigable rivers, lakes, &c.; secondly, by canals or rail roads, at the least expense of labor and capital. That city, then, that can be approached with exportable products with the least expense, will be the one naturally through which all the imports should come. To determine, then, the best system of trade for the whole population of every section, we must divide the country into its natural divisions, and assign to each its natural amount of business. If we establish our entire foreign and domestic trade on this natural basis, it will advance most rapidly the aggregate wealth and prosperity of the Union at large, and enable us in the shortest time to excel all other countries. The present population of the United States, on the Atlantic and gulf slope of the Rocky Mountains, have for their natural outlets cities or sites in Texas, Louisiana, Alabama, Florida, Georgia, the Carolinas, Virginia, Maryland, Pennsylvania, New York and Massachusett, also having natural limits to the amount of trade that for the interest of general population would naturally flow to them. At this time, the most important are Boston, New York, and Philadelphia, in the commercial and manufacturing States; Baltimore, Charleston, Mobile, New Orleans, and Galveston, are the most prominent in the agricultural States. In the two sections, there are Boston and New York as the principal outlets for the Northern and Eastern States, New Orleans and

Mobile as the most prominent natural outlets in the agricultural States. We annex table A, which shows the circulation of Bank paper in each State, the specie to redeem it, the exports and imports of each, their population, square miles, and public debt, an examination of which will readily show the most unnatural and injurious system of trade that could well exist amongst intelligent citizens living a government of equality and justice. This table at once shows that in the agricultural States all great interests are withering under the unnatural and extremely unhealthy system of our foreign trade. The cities in the Northern and Eastern States during the year ending June 30th, 1850, exported $70,249,809, and imported $155,291,737, showing that by our present system of trade they received over eighty-five millions imports, more than a natural system of trade would entitle them to.

The Southern and grain-growing Western States exported through their own ports $81,115,702, and imported $21,395,805, showing that they imported near sixty millions less than a proper trade would justify. On this large amount the consumers of foreign goods pay, to a great extent, importers' profits, jobber's profits, double shipping, storage, drayage and wharfage. The retail merchants spend double the time and money in going to make their purchases as would be necessary under a well regulated system of Direct Trade. Under this doubly expensive system, the retail merchants cannot sell foreign goods to consumers on an average at less than double the original foreign cost abroad.

The consumers of foreign goods in the Southern and Western States pay not less than twenty million of dollars annually more for their goods than would be necessary under a properly regulated system of Direct Trade. This twenty millions, however, is but a portion of the loss to the South and West. The Southern and Western States, as classed off in table A, make annually for export one hundred and fifty millions worth of produce, which, by the completion of a few of the rail roads now in progress would naturally find its way out at Southern ports, and by such a system as can and should be adopted by every Southern sea-port would, as soon as in full operation, put their import trade up to one hundred and fifty millions dollars, with all the advantageous consequences, to all classes of our citizens following such a change. Of what use are rail roads without freights and passengers? Where the necessity for Banks without a use for their circulation or accommodation? How can agriculture and manufactures prosper without commercial facilities? On reference to the table, it will be seen that New Orleans, which exports nearly as great an amount as New York, and should export double, only imports ten millions to New York one hundred and ten millions. As New Orleans and Mobile, and New York and Boston are the greatest ports naturally for the two sections, we will present a view of their trade and banking :

| | Exports. | Imports. | Bank Circulation. | Specie. |
|---|---|---|---|---|
| New Orleans and Mobile,.... | $48,650,208 | $11,625,861 | $7,386,000 | $8,503,000 |
| New York and Boston........ | 63,394,563 | 141,498,208 | 40,306,000 | 14,370,000 |

It appears from this statement, that while New Orleans and Mobile Bank capital is making about five per cent. on its specie, New York and Boston capital is making over twenty. For the ten years passed, New Orleans has not been able to keep ont as great a paper circulation as she had specie. New York and Boston, by their monopolising to a great extent the import trade, and consequently domestic trade, from artificial consequences, are also monopolising the profits on banking. As the heavy payments are due to New York and Boston, as fast as they make collections, should they be in Louisiana or Alabama bank paper, specie, or exchange on London, Liverpool, Boston, or New York is required, and their paper returned on them. As their paper is not, therefore, ultimately received in payment for debts due to New York and Boston, there is not the same demand for it as a circulating medium in the interior. But the amount of indebtedness being greatly beyond the natural limits of New York and Boston trade, and their Bank paper being received in payment, gives them more than their natural field of circulation. This applies to all the States of the Union that import less than their natural limits, as well as to Louisiana and Alabama.

As the proper adjustment of our foreign and domestic trade on the principles of economy laid down, involves the value of city, town, and country property, agricultural and manufacturing prosperity, the profits on bank, rail road and canal stocks, as well as population and political power, it becomes one of the highest consideration to all classes. To make the regulation properly and understandingly, it requires a very close scrutiny into every State and section of our widely extended country now settled.

The New England States are five in number. They contain 63,326 square miles, or a fraction over the size of Virginia. They are naturally by far the poorest five States in the Union as to soil, climate, mineral and vegetable productions. They contain a population of 2,727,397, engaged mostly in manufactures, commerce and the fisheries. A large majority of their citizens have for many years, been the advocates of high taxes, extravagant expenditures of the public funds, and government protection to favoured classes. The government allows them fishing bounties tonnage duties on their shipping, and protection to their domestic mannfactures. These advantages, with their large import trade, which naturally belongs to southern cities, with their industry and ingenuity and economy, have made them increase very rapidly in wealth and population. They have a contsitutional chronic infection of the *isms* which are as dangerous to good government and morality as Asiatic cholera to individuals; and more contagious. Their leading statesmen opposed the acquisition of Louisiana, Texas annexation and the Mexican war; have been in favor of confining our population to narrow limits, the consequence of which would be a reduction in wages of labor. Their fanatical opinions, with their desire of political power for sectional agrandisement, induces them to invite the foreign pauper population of Europe by millions to our shores, by proffering to give them the public lands that they deny the right of their southern brethren to purchase from the government and settle, only on degrading conditions of being ruled in their property by Mexican laws.

The other commercial and manufacturing States are, New Jersey, Pennsylvania, New York, Ohio and Michigan. They contain 197,027 square miles, and a population of 8,265,711. These States are much richer, naturally, than the New England States in vegetable and mineral productions. Iron ore, coal and copper is abundant; a large portion of them are productive in grain and vegetable productions common to cold climates. Agriculture, manufactures and commerce, all have a share of capital and labor devoted to their success. Commerce is the ruling interest, and in consequence of southern inattention, and the vigorous prosecution of that branch of industry and enterprise by New York, she has, to a great extent, monopolized the foreign and domestic trade of the Union. She spent forty millions on her canals, which are frequently closed with ice, and sixty millions on the New York and Erie, and other Rail Roads, to connect her with the Lake and Mississippi trade. These improvements, with her extensive foreign trade, has turned freights and passengers up stream in the Mississippi valley. Although her works of internal improvement cost a large amount, the advance on real estate in New York alone, will doubly pay the whole amount; besides rents, rail road and canal stocks, bank stocks and all interest are made to prosper in proportion to the extent of trade.

Before the revolutionary war, Virginia exported and imported three times more than New York, and had a greater population. New York now has thirty-three members in Congress and Virginia thirteen. In 1769, Virginia imported...... $4,085,472
The same year, New York imported........... 907,200
For the year ending 30th June, 1850, Virginia imported ................................ 426,399
New York imported.............................$111,123,524

This is a change in trade as remarkable as that in Hayti, produced by the abolition of African slavery. In 1789, Hayti exported 73,573,300 lbs. Mascavado sugar. The French, during their revolutionary days, abolished slavery. In 1840, under African free labor, Hayti exported 741 lbs. sugar.

The great change brought about in the trade of the northern and southern States has been caused by an almost exclusive application of capital and labor in the south, to agricultural pursuits; and the greater amount of capital and labor in the northern States being employed in commerce, internal improvements and manufactures, has given the northern people many millions annually of southern and western capital that could have been profitably employed in the south and west, which has enabled them to receive all the protection from the Federal Government for the encouragement of domestic manufactures, and tonage duties to build up commerce. In this manner the northern and New England sections has been receiving for many years, a constant flow of capital from the south and west, which, according to the best calculation that can be made, since 1808, has amounted in government protection, to nine hundred millions of dollars, and about a similar amount has been lost to the south and west in consequence of their indirect and expensive system of trade. Under this state of things the present prosperity of the commercial and manufacturing States is of very uncertain duration, as all unnatural systems of prosperity must be. Should the south and west, in the next five or ten years, embark extensively in commerce, internal improvements and manufactures, as it is clearly their interest to do, and the seat of commerce and manufactures be established in the most congenial parts of these sections, the present appearance of things will undergo a wonderful revolution. At this time the rapid progress of the various *isms* in the commercial and manufacturing States, must make the lovers of justice, order and good government, begin to feel the unhappy European uncertainty in the future. To accomplish the abolition of slavery is only one of the visionary dogmas of the day; the same principle will abolish rights to all property and all opinions not in accordance with its own. Unless this spirit is soon checked, the standing armies common in Europe, will soon be absolutely necessary in a number of the northern States. Mob law is already stronger than civil law. In a very considerable portion of New York, land rents cannot be regularly collected short of force of arms.

The commercial and manufacturing States owe a debt of $92,-154,118, which, if a healthy system of trade were established, would be at least four times, according to means, as great as that due by the agricultural States. A proper adjustment of the export and import trade would not give these States more than one-fourth of the Union.

The agricultural States are, Louisiana, Alabama, Mississippi, Arkansas, Texas, South Carolina, Georgia, Florida, North Carolina, Virginia, Maryland, Delaware, Tennessee, Kentucky, Missouri, Illinois, Indiana, Iowa and Wisconsin.

They contain an area of 1,043,686 square miles, which is four times as large as the commercial and manufacturing States, and nine times the size of Great Britain, and would at her density of population to the square mile, support two hundred millions of human beings. They contain now a population of twelve millions; lie in a compact body on the Atlantic and Gulf slope of the Rocky Mountains, with the great Mississippi river, making its way from the Lakes, through their centre, to the Gulf of Mexico, which is the great ocean river, sufficiently large to contain all the shipping of the world. Within their limits, are soils, climates, and seasons, capable of producing all the elements of food and raiment necessary for civilized man, in the greatest profusion; with timber sufficient to build all the boats, ships, steam vessels and houses that may be required for the next thousand years; water power more than sufficient to drive all the machinery of Europe and America; vast coal fields, inexhaustible for ages; iron ore, of the best quality, in the midst of the coal fields, to an extent that knows no limit, with thirty thousand miles steam boat navigation emptying into the Gulf and Atlantic at sufficient of points for all useful purposes; with more than two thousand miles of Sea and Gulf coast, never closed by ice, or even obstructed. This country is now the empire of agriculture.

In consequence of low grading and cheap right of way, rail roads can be built at one-third less cost, than in the commercial and manufacturing States; they will, therefore, be able to convey passengers and freights lower. The Mobile and Ohio, and Alabama and Tennessee River Rail Roads, commencing at Lake Michigan and Lake Erie, and terminating at the Bay of Mobile on the Gulf, will be to other roads what the Mississippi river is to other rivers. Mobile will, therefore, become the great outlet, by rail way, that New Orleans is, by water. The natural shape of the country points out the States of Illinois, Indiana, Kentucky, Missouri and Tennessee, the upper parts of Arkansas, Mississippi, and Alabama, as the heart of the rail road system, for this great slope or basin. This region will become the empire of manufactures. On the Gulf, where all the productions of this inexhaustible country, has a tendency to get an outlet, will become the empire of commerce. Here, at all seasons of the year, vessels can go and come by the assistance of the Gulf stream and trade winds. From the nature of things, these will be the great high ways of general commerce for centuries. One of the results of the war with Mexico, will be to turn the trade of the Pacific, to a great extent, across by the land route. Mobile and New Orleans will then be in a central position for extensive trade with surrounding countries. London and Liverpool, New York and Boston, will be far out on the outskirts.

Southern sea ports, not only have advantages of a back country containing all the natural elements in the highest degree of agricultural, commercial and manufacturing prosperity, but they have a population that renders more safety and stability to investments in any pursuit of life than any of the surrounding nations. None of the dangerous dogmas of the day can flourish in any of the slave or free States belonging to this division. Rights of property, according to our constitution, are strictly regarded and complied with without difficulty. They contain the best material for a defensive war of the age. A slave population, the most effective laborers for a warm climate, under the best discipline and most skillfnl direction of any other people, in numbers sufficient to raise the means of army subsistance for any probable war, too well fed, clothed and taken care of to be restless or unruly, and the least dangerous from insurrection. If the three millions of the African race now in these States were suddenly destroyed, millions of the white race in Europe and America would suffer for food and raiment. These States have a citizen army of over one million of freemen ready, without distinction of party, to defend their rights and liberties at the first call. With soils, climates and productions within their own limits, rendkring them entirely independent of the rest of mankind. They owe a public debt of $94,346,558, which, for their vast resources, is very small, their yearly surplus of exportable produce being one hundred and fifty millions dolllars worth.

Within the last fifty years they have reclaimed a vast wilderness from savage worthlessness, and converted it into cultivated fields of great usefulness to themselves and surrounding nations. Without government aid, they have excelled all other people in agriculture, now making an annual surplus to supply the wants of other nations, greater than any other country, regardless of extent of territory or numbers of laborers. At the same time they have paid a sum to build up commerce and mannfactures in an uncongenial clime, which spent economically within their own limits, would have made them first in commerce and manufactures as well as agriculture. They have enlighted, civilized, christianised and made useful to themselves and surrounding nations, a greater number of the African race than misguided philanthropy has or ever can do. Their vast agricultural productions,, if properly used, will enable them, without civil commotion or bloodshed, to preserve our peace and trauquility, our Union and liberty. Every patriotic citizen, then, within our country, should rally under our colors to battle in a common country's cause and the cause of mankind.

From a review of the whole subject, it is evident that the present unnatural concentration of commerce and manufactures in the northern and New England States, is a very great annual drawback on the aggregate wealth, prosperity, and progress of the Union. In consequeuce of its increasing their political power and thereby placing in their possession the direction of the Federal Government—under its influences at war with justice—the political equality of the citizens of the different States is destroyed, the protection of person and property by land and sea, guarantied to every citizen of every State and section defeated, the fundamental principles of our political compact annulled, and the harmony, tranquility and stability of the whole Union endangered. It is, therefore, the highest duty of every lover of our present form of government and stability of the Union, to make an exertion to create a natural and healthy system of agricultural, commercial and manufacturing pursuits throughout our extensive country. How can this be done in the shortest time, is the great question?

If we were to receive news that Great Britain was making every preparation within her power to prosecute a war upon us, to overthrow our present form of government and establish her system, we would all enter the great contest for the preservation of our rights, political and personal liberty. Troops would be called out from every State and territory. Our ablest officers would be placed in command. A force, according to the importance of the post, would be marched to every sea port. All our citizens, by every means in their power, would give aid and assistance to the armies. If an Arnold were found amongst us, unless he succeeded in making his escape, would be hung as high as Haman. What has been, we might reasonably expect again under similar circumstances. We know our armies, when well organised under able commanders, have proved victorious in every war against all odds of numbers. We know that a small army, composed of good material, well organised and skilfully commanded, can defeat many, indifferently organised and directed. Our policy in defending our coast would be to send a force able, on the first onset of the campaign, to gain a decisive victory, as that would inspire our forces and discourage the enemy.

It is true there is now no direct open war of arms against us, yet it requires no prophet to see in the present natural course of events, gradually and rapidly growing, one amongst the most bloody wars recorded on the pages of history. Individuals and nations at times are placed in circumstances that one false step decides their future existence. We now have it in our power, if we will at once seize the favorable opportunity, of gaining a great political victory—not by the shedding of brother's blood by brother, as Washington, Adams, Hancock, Jefferson, Franklin and their ever to be remembered compatriots were compelled to do, in order to secure political liberty—but by a commercial and manufacturing revolution, which instead of burthening us with heavy taxes, will annually advance our aggregate wealth by many millions.

On commencing this war, we find our opponents already fully organised and drilled; our own forces scattered over an extensive country, without any organization or discipline. To offset this, we find ourselves very favorably situated in one very important particular. We have their campaign provision, and our own, too, already in possession, which of course must decide the victory in our favor, if we are capable of properly using and successfully defending this important advantage. Their commercial and manufacturing prosperity now almost entirely rests upon our large surplus of exportable produce. We have been in the habit of letting them have the use of the greater portion of these exports without interest, and paying, double in profits and charges, which would be necessary, if conducted by our own citizens, through our own ports, on the most advantageous plan, to make our section bloom with prosperity. All then, that is required to ensure success, is to organise properly, a force competent in every way, to use our means for our own advantage, without letting them get the control as they have heretofore. This can be done best on mtlitary principles. Let every State raise an army of capitalists in numbers and amount, sufficient to carry every sea port on the coast at the first onset. This can be best done by getting the exports from, and amount of goods sold in the region of any port that can most conveniently obtain their supplies at such port. It is practicable under the system proposed. By incorporating the Alabamu Direct Trade and Exchange company, to lay down foreign goods in our cities, towns, villages, and landings, in proper quantities, lower than possibly can be done by New York and Boston, which will of course, take the trade. If the south and west, in this manner, revolutionize the trade of the country, they will change the relative sectional population, and, as a consequence, the political power. They have always been just and liberal to the north, and therefore if they had political power, would in all probability, use it with justice and liberality to all sections. We might then calculate that our country would move on rapidly to pre-eminence among nations. This is one side of the picture. There is another. By our conduct events may take a different turn. Sampson had power at one time to slay the Philistines, regardless of numbers. He was enticed from duty, bound while asleep, shorn of his locks of strength and his eyes put out. We are this day, physically, the most powerful people of the age; but there is a Delilah enticing us, deceptively in order that we may sleep until she binds us with a cord of free soil States, that our locks of strength may be shorn from us; which States, to a great extent, are to be reared up by the pauper population of Europe. They are now lean, lank, degraded, weakly human beings, entitled to our pity. When our lands, with the fat thereof, shall be divided amongst them, the change in their condition will be so sudden and great that they will know no limit to universal equality. Our fanatical neighbors, with the aid of a few foreign emissaries, can soon raise a crusade against their southern brethren on whose means they have been warmed into striking power. in the mean time our taxes will be increased; we will contribute millions to increase the wealth and power of another section. The love of power and sectional aggrandizement, aided by fanaticism, will encroach upon our dearest rights and liberties, until political and national death, under the circumstances, will be preferred to longer existence. The southern sword, seldom known to falter, will be drawn. Vigorously assaulted by cool, calculating power, and furiously assailed by fanaticism, attacked on all sides, by sea and by land, in front and rear, the deathly conflict will rage beyond a parrallel, until our common country will be drenched with blood from sea shore to mountain. Those who now fear to meet the gathering storm, and disperse or roll it back, may well then call on the rocks and mountains to fall upon them and hide them from their furious enemies. No human foresight can predict on which side victory will rest, but all can see a powerful check, a stop to civilization, progress, and well regulated human liberty on the North American Continent.

Every Southern sea-port city, except Baltimore, is doing an unnatural and less extensive import trade than would be entirely legitimate, and can add greatly to their own and the prosperity of the surrounding population by extending their commercial operations. Alabama and Louisiana, the one in Mobile, the other in New Orleans, each holds a great key to the future prosperity and progress of the millions of human beings that are to inhabit the

2

great Mississippi valley. In the present condition of the world, the cities above named are of vastly greater importance in a *pecuniary*, *political* and *military* point of view than Gibraltar, which is the key to the Mediterranean. After the adoption of the United States constitution, the possession of Louisiana by a foreign power and the consequent embarassments attending the free navigation of the Mississippi, threatened seriously the dissolution of the Union. In consequence of the modern system of railroads, Alabama holds a pass no less important than New Orleans. A failure to remove obstructions to free trade and travel through these important passes, leaves the population of Western Virginia and Ohio, Tennessee, Kentucky, Indiana, Michigan, Illinois, Iowa, Wisconsin, Missouri, Arkansas, a portion of Texas, and a vast territory back to the Rocky Mountains, as well as Louisiana and Alabama, with parts of other States, whose interest it is to have an outlet through the Gulf, practically in the same condition that a portion of the valley was before the acquisition of Louisiana. Access, the most perfect to each city from every direction, by land and water, is the true policy of the respective States to which they belong, and of the Union at large. The obstructions to a free access, to each city from all directions, consist in the shallowness of the channels at the mouth of the Mississippi, and of Mobile bay; they being too shallow to admit of large class vessels. But the greatest obstruction is that of the Iberville river, which is entirely obliterated for some distance in consequence of obstructions heretofore thrown into it. And also the want of postal lines making regular passages to and from important ports within our own limits and to foreign countries. There is also needed the completion of the main rail road trunks from the upper Mississippi valley to Mobile and New Orleans. The removal of these obstructions will properly come under national and State legislation for aid. Appropriations on the part of Congress will be within federal jurisdiction to an amount sufficient to deepen the mouth of the Mississippi and Mobile bay, so as to admit large class vessels; clear the Iberville river from obstructions that will permit a free passage of first class steamboats from the Mississippi into lake Ponchatrain. Appropriations of one hundred thousand dollars each, to four lines of steamers or other vessels, from Mobile to ports in Europe, South America, California, Asia and the Mediterranean, with the view of touching at all points on their respective routes desirable; appropriations of alternate sections of public lands in aid of a branch trunk of the Mobile and Ohio rail road to New Orleans; appropriations of lands in aid of the great rail road now in process of contruction from Lake Erie, by way of Cincinnati,

Ohio, Frankfort, Kentucky, Nashville, Tennessee, Selma in Alabama, to Mobile, connecting the Lakes with the Gulf; also, appropriations of alternate sections in aid of the two great railways now in process of construction, one connecting Memphis, Tennessee, with Charleston, South Carolina, and which is destined, as the country is settled, to progress until it reaches the Pacific coast; the other connecting Savannah, Georgia, with Vicksburg, Mississippi, will make its way through Texas.

Extensive bodies of public lands are now in Alabama unsold, and must remain government property many years, unless rail roads are constructed through them.

The rights and interests alike, of the citizens of the Mississippi valley and the Union, require the re-opening of Iberville river in the State of Louisiana, which formerly connected Lake Ponchatrain, by way of Lake Maurepas, with the Mississippi, at a short distance below the town of Baton Rouge. This river was formerly an open navigable stream, and of sufficient note to be recognized and established by the treaty of Paris in seventeen hundred and sixty three, as a part of the boundary line between the possessions of Great Britain and France. The Iberville river, at this period, was an outlet of the Mississippi, so large as to give the appellation of an island to that part of Louisiana on which New Orleans is situated; is now at its point of former efflux from that stream, entirely filled up and obliterated. It was open down to the period of the last war with Great Britain. During the war, General Jackson, for the common protection of the country, had obstructions thrown into it, under the impression that the enemy might attempt to pass through the lake and Iberville river into the Mississippi and fall upon New Orleans from above. As it is or was a natural highway, the citizens of the United States are entitled to its free use for purposes of navigation. As it was obstructed through the action of the *Federal government*, the same agency is bound to remove the obstructions. These obstructions all being removed and improvements completed, would be equivalent for all practical purposes, to placing each city on the Gulf stream, Mississippi river, and the great railways of the valley. A healthy city on the Gulf is necessary to draw off the upper Mississippi trade and travel from New York and Boston. The annual mortality, in proportion to population, is less in Mobile than New York. She can, therefore, so far as health is concerned, turn the business to the Gulf coast. New Orleans would then receive a greater trade and travel through Mobile than she ever will do, so long as the present system continues through New York and Boston. Louisiana is, therefore, interested in building up Mobile.

New York has expended over one hundred millions of dollars on rail roads and canals to carry the interior trade through her city. Alabama may now secure an outlet for, and an intercourse with, a region of greater extent, whose population can reach Mobile at a less expense than New York, by an outlay of capital, on the part of her citizens, individually, of one-fourth the sum New York has expended.

We annex a table which shows the number of railways in each State, miles in operation, and miles in course of construction, with the cost:

Table showing the extent of railways completed and under traffic, and capital invested in the different countries.

| | Miles. | Cost. |
|---|---|---|
| United Kingdom of Great Britain...... | 7,000 | £250,000,000 |
| German States.................. ... | 5,342 | 66,775,000 |
| United States........................ | 11,654 | 70,000,000 |
| France ............................ | 1,018 | 48 781,000 |
| Belgium ........................... | 532 | 9,576,000 |
| Russia ............................. | 600 | 9,000,000 |
| Italy ............................... | 170 | 3,000,000 |

## AGRICULTURAL STATES.

| STATES. | No. of Rail-ways. | Miles in operation. | Miles in course of construction. | Cost. |
|---|---|---|---|---|
| Delaware ............. | 1 | 16 | | 600,000 |
| Maryland............. | 3 | 255 | 172 | 14,220,503 |
| Virginia ............. | 16 | 485 | 735 | 8,930,421 |
| North Carolina.......... | 3 | 249 | 223 | 4,100,000 |
| South Carolina........ | 7 | 383 | 403 | 8,703,678 |
| Georgia .............. | 13 | 804 | 181 | 15,100,080 |
| Florida............... | 2 | 54 | 54 | 250,000 |
| Alabama ............. | 7 | 135 | 955 | 1,936,208 |
| Mississippi ........... | 4 | 100 | 518 | 1,770,000 |
| Louisiana ............ | 7 | 117 | 25 | 1,131,000 |
| Texas ................ | 1 | | 72 | |
| Tennessee ............ | 7 | 134 | 558 | 1,800,000 |
| Kentncky ............ | 6 | 93 | 446 | 1,751,226 |
| Indiana ............. | 20 | 538 | 1,117 | 9,690,000 |
| Michigan ............. | 4 | 474 | | 8,656,340 |
| Illinois ............... | 14 | 271 | 1,606 | 5,100,000 |
| Missouri .............. | 2 | 249 | 180 | |
| Iowa ................ | 1 | | | |
| Wisconsin ............ | 2 | 10 | 230 | 400,000 |
| Total ................ | 120 | 4,377 | 7,481 | $85,139,456 |

## COMMERCIAL AND MANUFACTURING STATES.

| STATES. | No. of Rail-ways. | Miles in operation. | Miles in course of construction. | Cost. |
|---|---|---|---|---|
| Maine .................. | 10 | 283 | 175 | $8,191,693 |
| New Hampshire........ | 16 | 463 | 76 | 14,144,755 |
| Vermont .............. | 9 | 369 | 167 | 13,116,553 |
| Massachusetts ........ | 37 | 1,153 | 67 | 51,884,572 |
| Rhode Island.......... | 1 | 50 | | 2,614,484 |
| Connecticut ........... | 13 | 510 | 64 | 18,198,599 |
| New York............ | 44 | 1,946 | 946 | 67,686,155 |
| Pennsylvania .......... | 51 | 1,323 | 535 | 49,662,918 |
| New Jersey........... | 10 | 290 | 40 | 7,445,000 |
| Ohio.................. | 26 | 890 | 1,481 | 17,066,661 |
| Total ................ | 217 | 7,277 | 3,551 | $250,012,410 |

Average cost per mile in Northern and N.England States,$37,500
Average cost in South and West.................... 19,600

In a military point of view, the importance of connecting New Orleans and Mobile with the interior States, by railway, considering the great number of rapid moving war steamers now belonging to various powers, cannot well be overestimated. In fifteen days time a large fleet of war steamers could cross the ocean and assail the two cities; their possession by an enemy would be disastrous to the interest of the valley population.

In the early history of Alabama, freights were conveyed on her rivers in flat boats and barges, propelled by manual labor. What son of hers would now be willing to abandon our floating palaces and return to the keels? Those who oppose rail roads advocate the same principle. There is, to accommodate our entire population, as great a necessity for rail roads with passenger and freight cars propelled by steam, instead of common wagons or coaches drawn by animal power, as there is for steamboats; and the average gain to the whole community, in trade and travel, is equally as great. Of course those who run boats where there are not freights and passengers sufficient to pay, will sink capital. Those who build rail roads where there should only run a plank or common wagon road, will do the same; those who plant on unproductive soils will be equally unfortunate.

The responsibility of Alabama at this time is exceedingly great. Her comamnding position requires deliberate and skillful action. She is now capable of doing much for herself and surrounding sisters. She is in a similar situation to many States of the Union, locally, that Mobile county is to a large number of counties in South Alabama and Eastern Mississippi. If there were no public high-way by land through Mobile county to the city, and many roads in other counties around seeking an outlet through her, and from indifference to her own prosperity and theirs, refuse to make an order for and open a road, she would soon be considered *foreign* in her position. The State can now have completed through her limits great railway lines of the first importance to her in every sense of the word, without doing anything more than endorse bonds that the companies of at least three of the roads, can secure her from final loss beyond a doubt. She is now in a situation to advance more rapidly, by proper action, every important interest within her limits, than any of the coast States from Maine to the Rio Grande. She has climate, soils, mineral and vegetable productions, with advantages from location, that render her second to no State in the Union, of the same area, in the great pursuits of agriculture, commerce and manufactures. The completion of the Mobile and Ohio, and the Alabama and Tennessee River Rail Roads, with others drawing in trade and travel from the east and west, would give to all her great interests, advantages that would enable them at least to keep pace with the most flourishing. She is capable of supporting a population double the five New England States, and half the capital and labor expended to build her up, that has been made to flow on them, will make her worth them all. She has a population of 771,071 on 50,722 squares miles; owes a public debt of $3,983,616; her principal city, Mobile, is at all seasons free from ice. Through the Gulf stream, trade winds, and Carribean sea, she is open to the trade of the world; subject to overflow from neither river or ocean; midway between the rich products of the tropics and the staple and provision growing States of the Mississippi valley; possessing one amongst the most healthy sites on the coast, with a harbor sufficient for the navies of the world, and room to build up a city equal in population to any on the Globe; backed, in the interior of the State, with extensive bodies of the most fertile lands; abundant water power, inexhaustible forests of timber, rich beds of iron ore and extensive coal fields in close proximity to each other, all in the midst of the cotton, sugar and grain growing regions. She requires no uncertain government protection to make her among the first in agriculture, commerce and manufactures. She is in a situation at this time, by a grand move on an extensive scale, in commerce, on principles of proper economy, to make all her great interests bound forward with unusual rapidity. If the surrounding States continue their unprofitable and dependant policy, Alabama should only embark the more rapidly and to a greater extent. Under such circumstances, with the necessary capital and skill, one more generation would find her in this great group of States, what New York is to the thirty named. During the year 1850, there were sold in Alabama, sixteen millions dollars worth of merchandize ; of this sum not less than eight millions were foreign, nearly all imported through northern cities, taxed to a great extent with double profits, drayage, storage and insurance. Under such a system of trade, the retail merchants cannot furnish consumers of foreign goods at less than one hundred per cent. on original cost, which would leave four millions as the foreign cost of our imported merchandize. Under a well regulated system of direct trade, this four millions would go into consumers hands at six millions five hundred thousand dollars and leave as great a profit to the merchant as he now receives, and save one million five hundred thousand dollars to consumers, a sum equal, annually, to three years taxes. The bill under consideration proposes to accomplish this by incorporating a limited partnership in the shape of a joint stock company, composed of capitalist and business men in all parts of the country, with power to own ships, boats or vessels, buy and sell produce and manufactures at home and abroad on commission, receive and pay out deposits, deal in foreign and domestic exchange generally, make advances on produce, manufactures and merchandize, and to increase their capital stock, if necessary, to three millions of dollars.

For the protection of the community against abuses, the officers and directrs are required to make bonds and take suitable oaths for the faithful performance of their duties; make annual reports showing who are the stockholders, the amount of each one's shares and the true condition of the company. The bill also enables the Governor to appoint commissioners to examine the entire business of the company, and report thereon publicly. If the company abuses its powers, the legislature can annul their charter.

Well organised with competent agencies at different foreign and domestic points of trade, they would not only be highly useful to the mercantile and planting community in making their sales, purchases and exchanges, but could also, to great advantage, make purchases at home and abroad of materials or machinery for our rail road and manufacturing companies.

## IMPORTS INTO THE UNITED STATES FROM, AND EXPORTS TO, FOREIGN COUNTRIES, FOR YEAR ENDING JUNE 30, 1850.

| COUNTRIES. | Value of imports. | Value of Exports. | | |
|---|---|---|---|---|
| | | Domestic Produce. | Foreign Produce. | Total. |
| Russia | $1,511,572 | $666,435 | $198,506 | $864,941 |
| Prussia | 27,469 | 70,645 | 27,991 | 98,636 |
| Sweden and Norway | 1,032,117 | 668,580 | 51,610 | 720,190 |
| Denmark | 527 | 165,874 | 20,706 | 186,580 |
| Hanse Towns | 8,787,874 | 4,320,780 | 885,740 | 5,206,522 |
| Holland | 1,686,967 | 2,188,101 | 416,564 | 2,604,665 |
| Dutch Guiana | 71,043 | 97,014 | 56,683 | 102,439 |
| Belgium | 2,404,954 | 2,168,357 | 5,425 | 2,543,760 |
| England | 72,118,971 | 64,686,959 | 4,210,271 | 68,897,230 |
| Scotland | 2,746,670 | 3,021,740 | 183,679 | 3,205,419 |
| Ireland | 293,783 | 1,025,031 | 42,693 | 1,067,724 |
| Gibraltar | 44,269 | 186,307 | 60,482 | 246,789 |
| Malta | 11,354 | 75,329 | 39,051 | 114,380 |
| Cape of Good Hope | 72,206 | 143,219 | ........ | 143,219 |
| Honduras | 178,690 | 171,984 | 16,551 | 188,535 |
| British Guiana | 14,591 | 502,776 | 22,663 | 525,439 |
| Canada | 4,285,470 | 4,641,451 | 1,289,370 | 5,930,821 |
| British American Colonies | 1,358,992 | 3,116,840 | 501,374 | 3,618,214 |
| Other British possessions | 497 | ........ | ........ | ........ |
| France | 27,538,025 | 17,950,277 | 1,883,070 | 19,833,347 |
| Miquelon and French Fisheries | ........ | 2,517 | ........ | 2,517 |
| French Guiana | 12,551 | 43,405 | 1,382 | 44,787 |
| Bourbon | 10,005 | 12,575 | 2,200 | 14,775 |
| Spain | 2,082,395 | 3,862,021 | 125,413 | 3,987,434 |
| Teneriffe and other Canaries | 85,223 | 20,524 | 5,065 | 25,589 |
| Manilla and Phillipine Islands | 1,336,866 | 16,817 | 1,450 | 18,267 |
| Portugal | 339,763 | 172,978 | 5,236 | 178,214 |
| Madeira | 114,729 | 136,874 | 6,527 | 143,401 |
| Fayal and other Azores | 16,328 | 14,421 | 2,152 | 16,573 |
| Cape de Verde Islands | ........ | 47,043 | 2,167 | 49,210 |
| Italy | 2,105,077 | 1,567,166 | 239,904 | 1,807,070 |
| Sicily | 822,629 | 50,577 | 13,024 | 63,601 |
| Sardinia | 205 | 170,764 | 86,136 | 256,900 |
| Tuscany | ........ | 45,664 | 23,468 | 69,132 |
| Trieste and other Austrian ports | 467,601 | 1,179,893 | 312,111 | 1,492,004 |
| Turkey | 801,023 | 204,397 | 53,344 | 257,741 |
| Mexico | 2,135.366 | 1,498,791 | 514.036 | 2,012,827 |
| Central America | 261,459 | 57,225 | 12,967 | 70,192 |
| New Grenada | 591,992 | 970,619 | 285,600 | 1,256,219 |
| Venezuela | 1,920.247 | 678,461 | 340,008 | 1,018,470 |
| Brazil | 9,324,429 | 2,723,767 | 473,347 | 3,197,114 |
| Argentine Republic | 2,653,877 | 718,331 | 346,311 | 1,064,642 |
| Cisplatine Republic | ........ | 60,024 | 1,518 | 61,542 |
| Chili | 1,796,877 | 1,297,133 | 125,588 | 1,422,721 |
| Peru | 170,753 | 258,939 | 16,789 | 275,728 |
| China | 6,593,462 | 1,485,961 | 119,256 | 1,605,217 |
| West Indies | 26,209,200 | 16,367,345 | 1,368,056 | 17,891,201 |
| East Indies | 3,349,420 | 683,146 | 419,798 | 1,102,944 |
| South America generally | 86,659 | 22,256 | 50,442 | 72,698 |
| Asia generally | 402,599 | 315,463 | 13,321 | 328,784 |
| Africa generally | 524,722 | 730,932 | 28,334 | 759,266 |
| South Sea Islands | ........ | 169,025 | 20,837 | 189,862 |
| Equador | 4,618 | 24,414 | 10,511 | 34,925 |
| Total | $178,079,818 | $136,946,912 | $14,951,808 | $151,898,720 |

## MERCHANDIZE SOLD IN ALABAMA DURING THE YEAR 1850.

| Counties. | Amount. |
|---|---|
| ıtauga | $110,225 00 |
| .rbour | 535,737 00 |
| .ldwin | 18,911 00 |
| nton | 143,665 00 |
| bb | 73,921 00 |
| ount | 24,457 00 |
| ıtler | 85,432 00 |
| ıambers | 228,364 00 |
| ıerokee | 90,350 00 |
| ıoctaw | 49,705 00 |
| arke | 39,237 00 |
| offee | 48,296 00 |
| onecuh | 66,655 00 |
| oosa | 475,847 00 |
| ovington | 8,602 00 |
| ale | 26,514 00 |
| allas | 505,430 00 |
| eKalb | 37,810 00 |
| ıyette | 26,220 00 |
| 'anklin | 277,515 00 |
| reene | 403,407 00 |
| enry | 185,527 00 |
| ıckson | 77,481 00 |
| ıuderdale | 236,000 00 |
| ıwrence | 117,697 00 |
| imestone | 166,014 00 |
| owndes | 169,043 00 |
| acon | 279,855 00 |
| adison | 382,692 00 |
| arshall | 82,066 00 |
| arengo | 232,038 00 |
| arion | 27,086 00 |
| obile | 6,774,867 00 |
| onroe | 134,332 00 |
| ontgomery | 1,675,211 00 |
| organ | 107,244 00 |
| erry | 348,726 00 |
| ickens | 180,888 00 |
| ike | 45,483 00 |
| andolph | 48,386 00 |
| ussell | 48,863 00 |
| helby | 71,499 00 |
| t. Clair | 53,826 00 |
| umter | 322,997 00 |
| alladega | 226,251 00 |
| allapoosa | 54,600 00 |
| uscaloosa | 454,078 00 |
| Valker | 28,433 00 |
| Vashington | 2,801 00 |
| Vilcox | 145,045 00 |
| Total | $16,020,976 00 |

# STATEMENT,

Showing the number of Banks, their Circulation and Specie, together with the Exports, Imports, Population, Representatives, Public Debt, and Square Miles of each State, for the year ending June 30, 1850.

## AGRICULTURAL STATES.

| STATES. | No. of Banks. | Circulation. | Specie. | Exports. | Imports. | Population | No. Representatives. | Public Debt | Sq. miles. |
|---|---|---|---|---|---|---|---|---|---|
| Louisiana | 5 | $4,200,000 | $7,300,000 | $38,205,350 | $10,760,499 | 500,763 | 4 | $11,492,656 | 46,481 |
| Alabama | 2 | 3,186,000 | 1,203,422 | 10,544,858 | 865,362 | 771,671 | 7 | 3,983,616 | 50,722 |
| Mississippi | 1 | | | | | 592,853 | 5 | 7,271,707 | 47,156 |
| Arkansas | | | | | | 209,639 | 2 | 1,506,562 | 52,198 |
| Texas | 1 | | | 24,958 | 25,650 | 187,403 | 2 | 2,435,982 | 237,321 |
| South Carolina | 14 | 6,090,000 | 2,200,000 | 11,447,800 | 1,933,785 | 668,507 | 5 | 2,061,292 | 24,500 |
| Georgia | 17 | 1,000,000 | 1,600,000 | 7,551,943 | 636,994 | 905,999 | 8 | 1,828,472 | 58,000 |
| Florida | | | | 2,623,624 | 95,709 | 87,387 | 1 | | 59,268 |
| North Carolina | 19 | 3,500,000 | 1,600,000 | 416,501 | 323,692 | 868,903 | 8 | 977,000 | 45,000 |
| Virginia | 35 | 7,000,000 | 2,300,000 | 3,415,646 | 426,599 | 1,421,081 | 13 | 15,196,856 | 61,352 |
| Maryland | 24 | 3,268,000 | 1,500,000 | 6,967,353 | 6,124,201 | 583,035 | 6 | 15,424,380 | 9,856 |
| Delaware | 9 | 900,000 | 250,000 | | | 91,535 | 1 | | 2,120 |
| Teneessee | 21 | 4,000,000 | 1,500,000 | | 27,966 | 1,002,625 | 10 | 3,352,856 | 45,600 |
| Kentucky | 23 | 6,680,000 | 2,680,000 | | | 982,405 | 10 | 4,397,637 | 37,680 |
| Missouri | 6 | 2,600,000 | 1,900,000 | | 359,643 | 682,043 | 7 | 922,261 | 67,380 |
| Illinois | | | | 17,669 | 15,705 | 858,298 | 9 | 16,627,509 | 55,405 |
| Indiana | 14 | 3,300,800 | 1,280,000 | | | 988,734 | 11 | 6,775,522 | 33,809 |
| Iowa | 1 | | | | | 192,214 | 2 | 79,442 | 50,914 |
| Wisconsin | | | | | | 304,226 | 3 | 12,892 | 58,924 |
| Total of Agricultural States | 192 | $45,724,800 | $25,313,422 | $81,115,702 | $21,395,805 | 11,899,321 | 114 | $94,346,558 | 1,048,686 |

# STATEMENT,

Showing the number of Banks, their Circulation and Specie, together with the Exports, Imports, Population, Representatives, Public Debt, and Square Miles in each State, for the year ending June 30, 1850.

## COMMERCIAL AND MANUFACTURING STATES.

| STATES. | No. of Banks | Circulation. | Specie. | Exports. | Imports. | Population | No. Representatives. | Public Debt | Sq. miles. |
|---|---|---|---|---|---|---|---|---|---|
| Michigan | 6 | $650,000 | $116,000 | $132,045 | $144,102 | 397,654 | 4 | $2,529,872 | 56,243 |
| Ohio | 57 | 10,366,000 | 2,750,000 | 217,632 | 582,504 | 1,977,031 | 21 | 18,744,594 | 39,964 |
| New York | 190 | 24,400,000 | 11,620,000 | 52,712,800 | 111,123,524 | 3,090,022 | 33 | 23,463,838 | 46,000 |
| New Jersey | 25 | 2,900,000 | 690,000 | 1,165 | 1,494 | 489,333 | 5 | 71,810 | 8,820 |
| Pennsylvania | 38 | 7,000,000 | 2,500,000 | 4,049,464 | 12,066,154 | 2,311,681 | 25 | 40,316,362 | 46,000 |
| | 316 | $45,316,000 | $17,676,000 | $57,113,106 | $123,917,778 | 8,265,711 | 88 | $85,126,476 | 197,027 |
| Maine | 32 | $2,300,000 | $424,000 | $1,556,912 | $856,411 | 583,088 | 6 | $600,500 | 30,000 |
| Massachusetts | 124 | 15,900,000 | 2,750,000 | 10,681,763 | 30,374,684 | 994,499 | 11 | 6,259,930 | 7,800 |
| Connecticut | 27 | 2,300,000 | 120,000 | 241,930 | 372,390 | 370,791 | 4 | 91,212 | 4,674 |
| New Hampshire | 22 | 1,700,000 | 150,000 | 8,927 | 49,079 | 317,864 | 3 | 76,000 | 9,280 |
| Rhode Island | 38 | 1,100,000 | 130,000 | 216,265 | 258,303 | 147,544 | 2 | .......... | 1,360 |
| Vermont | 27 | 2,300,000 | 120,000 | 430,906 | 463,092 | 313,611 | 3 | .......... | 10,212 |
| | 270 | $25,600,000 | $3,694,000 | $13,136,703 | $32,373,959 | 2,727,397 | 29 | $7,027,642 | 63,326 |
| | 316 | 45,316,000 | 17,676,000 | 57,113,106 | 123,917,779 | 8,265,711 | 88 | 85,126,476 | 197,027 |
| Total Commercial and Manufacturing States | 586 | $69,916,000 | $21,370,000 | $70,249,809 | $155,291,737 | 10,993,008 | 117 | $92,154,118 | 260,353 |

The basis of foreign commercial exchanges rightfully belonging to the Agricultural States, as classed in the foregoing report, consists mainly in exports of Cotton, Tobacco, Rice, and Breadstuffs. The following table shows the amount of each for a series of years, exclusive of Rice :

| Year. | Cotton consumed in U. States. | Exports to Foreign Countries. | | | |
|---|---|---|---|---|---|
| | | Cotton. | Breadstuffs. | Tobacco. | Total. |
| 1843.. | ............. | $49,000,000 | $11,000,000 | ............. | ............. |
| 1844.. | $13,000,000 | 54,000,000 | 18,000,000 | ............. | ............. |
| 1845.. | 11,000,000 | 51,000,000 | 17,000,000 | ............. | ............. |
| 1846.- | 13,000,000 | 42,000,000 | 28,000,000 | ............. | ............. |
| 1847.. | 17,000,000 | 53,000,000 | 69,000,000 | $7,000,000 | $129,000,000 |
| 1848.. | 14,000,000 | 62,000,000 | 37,000,000 | 8,000,000 | 107,000,000 |
| 1849.. | 15,000,000 | 66,000,000 | 39,000,000 | 6,000,000 | 101,000,000 |
| 1850.. | 22,000,000 | 72,000,000 | 26,000,000 | 10,000,000 | 108,000,000 |
| 1851.. | 20,000,000 | 98,000,000 | 25,000,000 | 10,000,000 | 133,000,000 |

The basis of foreign commercial exchanges rightfully belonging to the Manufacturing and Commercial States, as classed in the foregoing statement, consists mainly in their exports of Manufactures and Fisheries; and the following table shows the aggregate amount in round numbers for a series of years, together with the Revenue collected by the Government :

| Year. | Exports of Manufactures. | Exports of Fisheries. | Total. | Revenue collected by U. States |
|---|---|---|---|---|
| 1840..... | $10,000,000 | $720,000 | $10,720,000 | ............. |
| 1841..... | 10,000,000 | 751,000 | 10,751,000 | ............. |
| 1842..... | 8,000,000 | 730,000 | 8,730,000 | ............. |
| 1843..... | 7,000,000 | 497,000 | 7,497,000 | ............. |
| 1844..... | 9,000,000 | 897,000 | 10,397,000 | $28,504,519 |
| 1845..... | 10,000,000 | 1,000,000 | 11,000,000 | 29,769,134 |
| 1846..... | ............. | ............. | ............. | 29,499,217 |
| 1847..... | 12,000,000 | 3,000,000 | 15,000,000 | 26,346,790 |
| 1848..... | 15,000,000 | 1,980,000 | 16,980,000 | 35,436,750 |
| 1849..... | 14,000,000 | 2,547,000 | 16,547,000 | 31,074,347 |
| 1850..... | 14,000,000 | ............. | ............. | 43,375,798 |
| 1851..... | ............. | ............. | ............. | 52,000,000 |

## A BILL

To be entitled An Act to incorporate the Alabama Direct Trade and Exchange Company.

SEC. 1. *Be it enacted by the Senate and House of Representatives of the State of Alabama in General Assembly convened*, That R. F. Houston, John C. Whitsitt, Duke W. Goodman, Charles LeBaron, Price Williams, William R. Cunningham, James M. Wallace, John W. Bush, James B. Gladney, Thomas B. Gardner, John A. Boyd, Daniel Turnipseed, John Moore, James B. Wallace, William Garrett and George G. Henry, and their associates and successors, or assigns, are hereby formed and created a body corporate by the name and style of "The Alabama Direct Trade and Exchange Company;" by which name they may sue and be sued, plead and be impleaded in all matters of law and equity whatever. They are hereby made capable of owning by purchase, or otherwise, ships, steam vessels, property, and effects, whether land, goods, money or choses in action, and to sell, exchange or otherwise dispose of the same, as natural persons may. They may have a common seal, and the same break, alter or amend at pleasure. They may make by-laws and ordinances for their own proper government, as they may choose: *Provided*, The same be not violative of the constitution or laws of this State, nor those of the United States. They may establish, on their own account, agencies in this State or any other State in the Union, and in foreign countries, for the purposes of facilitating a direct trade; receive, ship and sell the produce, merchandize, and manufactures of this or other States of the Union, abroad, and in like manner import into this States, from foreign markets, the produce, merchandize, or manufactures of foreign countries, and deal generally in foreign and domestic bills of exchange, and may receive commissions such as may be reasonable or agreed upon for the same. They may make advances on shipments and charge interest and commissions thereon, and may do and transact all business as is, or may become necessary, for carrying on a business of the kind. Said company shall not purchase or own, on its own account, any property, or ship, or import any article for its own use, except such as is necessary in carrying on its business, or is taken for the purpose of securing debts due said company; but shall confine themselves strictly and in good faith to the commission business contemplated by this act. And the stockholders are liable for the debts and defaults of said company, in proportion and to the extent only of the stock subscribed in their individual capacities, in addition to the strict liabilities of the company as such.

SEC. 2. *And be it further enacted*, That the company shall not be considered organised until the members thereof shall have subscribed stock, in shares of one hundred dollars each to the amount of two hundred thousand dollars, and there shall have been paid in for the use of said company twenty thousand dollars in gold or silver coin of the United States. Other persons may be admitted as members, from time to time, by a vote of two-thirds of the members at the time, allowing one vote for each five shares; but the capital stock may, in the same manner, be increased to not exceeding three millions of dollars.

SEC. 3. *And be it further enacted*, That the affairs of said company shall be managed by a Pesident and five Directors, to be styled "The Board of President and Directors;" which officers shall be elected by the stockholders annually, beginning on such day as they may appoint, and voting five shares to the vote, as aforesaid. It shall be the duty of an agent or member of said company to sell or dispose of, according to order, all produce, merchandize, &c., consigned to said company by citizens of the United States; and another agent or member of said company, to sell or dispose of that which may be consigned to said company by citizens of foreign countries. One agent or member, at least, of said company shall reside abroad, with a view to making or superintending purchases ordered through said company. Clerks, agents, and other officers necessary, may be elected by the President and Directors, who may require them to take an oath, and to give bonds such as they may prescribe, &c.

SEC. 4. *Be it further enacted*, That the President and Directors, members, or agents, acting as aforesaid, shall, before entering upon the duties of their office, each take and subscribe, before some Justice of the peace, an oath, as follows: "I, as President, agent, or Director, &c., of the 'Alabama Direct Trade and Exchange Company,' do solemnly swear that I will sell or purchase, or cause to be sold or purchased, any produce or commodity whatever, entrusted for that purpose to said company, to the best advantage to the owner thereof, and whatever I do in reference thereto shall be with a view to his best interest; and faithfully discharge all other duties of my office. So help me God. Signed, this ——————————." Said officers shall also each, aforesaid, enter into a bond, with security, in such sum as the stockholders may prescribe, payable to the Governor of the State, and his successors in office, and conditioned faithfully to perform the duties of his office, [naming it,] and to do all things in connection therewith according to the best snterest of the employers and patrons of said company. Said bonds may be sued upon by any one injured, but this shall not diminish any other right or remedy which any person may have against any such officer of the company. Said bonds shall be approved by and filed in the office of the Judge of Probate of Mobile county, with the offidavits above named.

Sec. 5. *Be it further enacted*, That the shares of stock in this company are transferable under such regulations as the Directory may prescribe; but in case of a failure of the company within six mouths after the transfer, the party selling, as well as the purchaser, shall be liable for the debts of the company in proportion to the stock transferred only; and said directory may make rules preventing the transfer of shares by a stockholder indebted to the company, as well as to withhold dividends from delinquents.

[Section 6, granting summary process of collections for and against the company, was stricken out by the Senate.]

Sec. 7. *Be it further enated*, That accounts of sales and other transactions of said company must be promptly made up and kept, and statements furnished to persons interested immediately by mail or otherwise, or within ten days, if the transaction is in thiscountry; if abroad, being forwarded with like promptitude, must be furnished within ten days after their reception at the office in this country: and on failure to comply with this provision, the company is held liable to pay any one interested the sum of one hundred dollars, to be recovered on motion after notice, as above stated.

Sec. 8. *Be it further enacted*, That said company shall at no time create or have outstanding obligations for an amount greater than the amount of capital stock actually paid in and two-thirds the cash value of produce, manufactures, &c., on hand at the time; and if so, the President and Directors acting at the time, are held liable in their individual capacities for losses which may ensue in consequence thereof; nor does this diminish or impair any other right or remedy against the company. So also are the President and Directors liable in their natural and individual capacities if they draw on produce or merchandize entrusted to them, and which the owners have not drawn on, so as in any way to make a forced and sacrificing sale by them necessary. But the President or any of the Directory may exonerate themselves by calling a meeting, which they, for that purpose, have a right to do immeciately, and give notice that they were absent at the time such excess or irregularity occurred, or that they dissented from it at the time, and the same must be entered on the books of the company.

Sec. 9. *Be it further enacted*, That unless this company commence the operation of direct trade and importations from abroad within five years, or if said company at any time cease to carry on a direct trade, as herein contemplated, and do not in good faith adhere to the provisions and objects of this charter, then the legislature may, at any session, repeal this act.

Sec. 10. *And be it further enacted*, That said company, previous to the meeting of the legislature, shall make to the Governor a complete report of their transactions, showing the amount of their assets and liabilities, and of what they consist, a list of the stockholders, and the shares held by each. The Governor may also, if he deem it necessary, biennially, or oftener, if he choose, appoint three Commissioners to examine into the condition of the affairs ef said company; said commissioners shall be furnished by the company with their books, papers, &c., and have extended to them every facility for a full and thorough examination; they shall receive for their services, to be paid by the company, three dollars per day, for not exceeding fifteen days. and make report to the Governor; they shall also take and subscribe an oath that they had not previously to the time of said examinntion, communicated to the company the time when they would commence.

www.ingramcontent.com/pod-product-compliance
Lightning Source LLC
LaVergne TN
LVHW011133110826
845150LV00008B/2317

* 9 7 8 1 4 1 8 1 9 4 3 6 9 *